© 1996 Geddes & Grosset Ltd
Published by Geddes & Grosset Ltd,
New Lanark, Scotland.

ISBN 1 85534 165 4

Printed and bound in UK

10 9 8 7 6 5 4 3 2

The Birth of Jesus

Retold by Judy Hamilton
Illustrated by Lindsay Duff

Tarantula Books

Long ago in the land of the Jews, in a little town called Nazareth, there lived a young woman called Mary. She had been brought up by her parents to know about God, to believe in him and to love him. Mary was betrothed to a man called Joseph, who was a carpenter.

In those days, the country was ruled by the Romans, and the Jews were unhappy as the Romans made them obey laws that they did not believe in. They longed to be free and to call the land their own again. God had promised them that one day he would send them a Saviour who would free them and reign over them in goodness and peace. Mary, like all the other Jewish people, longed for that special day to come.

One day, while Mary was alone, an Angel of God came to her. Mary was very frightened, but the Angel told her not to be afraid, for God had chosen her for a special honour.

"You are going to have a baby," the Angel told Mary. "The baby will be called Jesus, and he will be the Son of God, sent to reign over the world."

Mary was quite stunned by this news, but she loved God and so she told the Angel that she would do whatever God asked of her.

The Angel appeared before Joseph as well and told him that Mary was to become the mother of the Son of God. Joseph vowed to look after her as best he could. Mary and Joseph were soon married and looked forward to the miraculous birth.

One day, when Mary was nearly ready to give birth, an announcement was made in the town that the Roman emperor, Caesar Augustus, had ordered all the Jewish men to go to the towns of their birth, to register their names for a census. Caesar Augustus wanted to make sure that everybody paid the new taxes which he was forcing upon them.

Joseph, unlike Mary, did not come from Nazareth. He had been born in Bethlehem, a long way away. He did not like to make Mary travel so far when she was so close to giving birth, but he knew that he had no choice, and they soon set off on the long and difficult journey. Joseph walked while Mary rode along on a donkey beside him.

It took Mary and Joseph several days to reach Bethlehem. When they finally arrived, late one night, they were both very tired. Mary realized that her baby was ready to be born, and so they began to look for a place where they could spend the night and where the baby could be born in safety.

But this was not so easy as Bethlehem was full of people from other towns, ordered there for the census, just as Mary and Joseph had been.

They were beginning to despair of finding a place when a kindly innkeeper took pity on them. He showed them to a stable beside the inn and told them that they could rest there for the night. Mary and Joseph wearily thanked him for his kindness and settled down among the animals.

And so it was, that in the middle of the night, Mary of Nazareth gave birth to Jesus, the Son of God, in the stable, surrounded by animals. She had no cradle for him, so she carefully wrapped him in swaddling clothes and laid him gently down in a wooden manger full of straw to keep him warm and comfortable. No one could ever have guessed that such an important child would come into the world in such a humble way.

The animals in the stable stared at the baby as if in wonderment. They seemed to know that this was a special child. And outside, high up in the sky, there shone a star brighter than anyone had ever seen before. This was God's sign to the world that he had sent his Son to be their Saviour

Inside the stable, the Baby Jesus settled sweetly to sleep with his parents watching over him and the oxen lowing gently beside him.

But not everybody was asleep that night. Out on the hillside above the town of Bethlehem, there were some shepherds, watching over their flocks of sheep to protect them from wolves and thieves in the darkness. As they sat there quietly under the stars, they suddenly saw a brilliant flash of light, so bright that it almost blinded them. Through the light, an Angel of God appeared in front of the shepherds. The shepherds had never seen such a thing before and fell trembling to their knees. But the Angel spoke to the terrified men, calming their fears.

"Do not be afraid," the Angel said, "for I have wonderful news to tell you."

The shepherds listened.

"It is news of great joy for the whole world," said the Angel. "In Bethlehem today there has been born a baby, a Saviour for all people, called Christ the Lord. And this is how you will know him. You will be able to find the baby, wrapped in swaddling clothes, lying in a manger."

When the shepherds heard these words, they felt tremendous joy. Then the sky suddenly filled with a multitude of Angels, singing songs of praise to God.

The shepherds began at once to make their way down to Bethlehem to find the Saviour.

It was just as the Angel had said. When the shepherds arrived in Bethlehem, they soon found the stable beside the inn. Inside lay the Baby Jesus, sleeping in the manger of the stable. The shepherds fell down on their knees to worship him and to give thanks to God for his precious gift to the world.

Filled with joy at having seen the Son of God, the shepherds left to go and spread the wonderful news that the Angel had brought.

Meanwhile, in the stable, Mary sat beside her son, thinking of all that had happened. This baby was not for her alone. He was far too special. Mary had been chosen to give birth to the baby whom God was giving to the whole of mankind. She could have him to herself for a while, but not for long.

Far away in the lands of the East, there lived three Wise Men. Prophets had told them of a King who would be born in Bethlehem and who would reign over the Jews. When the Wise Men saw the bright star that shone in the sky they knew it was a sign from God and followed it. Soon they arrived in Jerusalem, and began to ask people:

"Where is the baby who has been born King of the Jews? We have come to worship him."

King Herod, in his palace nearby, heard that the Wise Men were searching for a new King. He was angry. Was *he* not King of the Jews?

He summoned the Wise Men and told them:

"When you find the baby, come and tell me where he is. I would like to worship him too."

The Wise Men travelled on that night towards Bethlehem, with the star in the sky to guide them. The star led them to the humble stable in which Jesus lay. They went into the stable and at once they bowed before the Holy Child, worshipping him and giving thanks to God. They had each brought a special gift for Jesus, and they humbly offered them to him – precious gold, sweet-smelling incense and myrrh. Then they left, filled with joy at the wonderful things they had seen.

The Wise Men had been told by King Herod to tell him where he could find the new King, but as they slept that night, God told them not to go back to Jerusalem, and in the morning they set off to return to their own lands another way.

Mary and Joseph stayed in Bethlehem for one more day. But that night Joseph was visited by the Angel again.

"You must flee to Egypt," said the Angel. "King Herod will come looking for the child and will try to kill him."

Joseph knew that the Angel spoke the truth. Gently, he woke Mary and told her what they must do. Packing up their belongings once more and lifting Jesus from his manger bed, Mary and Joseph set out on the long journey to safety in Egypt.

Herod was angry. When he could not find the baby King, he did the most terrible thing. He ordered all boys in Bethlehem under the age of two to be killed. It was a very sad time.

In time, the wicked King Herod died. The Angel appeared before Joseph and spoke to him again:

"The man who wished to see the child dead is no longer alive," said the Angel. "Take your wife and the child back to Israel once more."

So Joseph took his family back to Israel, but he did not return to Bethlehem or Jerusalem. Herod's son, Archelaus, now ruled as king there. God had warned Joseph that it was not safe to go there. Instead, Joseph took his family back to the little town of Nazareth. Joseph went back to working as a carpenter and the Boy Jesus, carefully watched over by his loving parents, lived out the rest of the first chapter of his life in safety and peace.